ONE PART NONSENSE

By Julia Anshasi

Giant Publishing Company
Lincoln, Nebraska, USA

2020 by Julia Anshasi

Published by Giant Publishing Company
Post Office Box 6455
Lincoln, NE 68506
www.giantpublishingcompany.com

Printed in the United States of America

Library of Congress Cataloging-in-Publication Data
Anshasi, Julia, 1963 -
One Part Nonsense/Contemporary humor/Julia Anshasi
    1. Humor
    2. Fiction

TXu002208003   2020

ISBN 978-1-7352827-0-1

Books by Julia Anshasi

Broken ~ Poems from the Holy Spirit
Copyright 2017 – Winner of the 2021 Illumination Book Awards Silver Medal

Some Things are HOT! Some Things are NOT!
Copyright 2018

Behind the Word: Bible Stories to Ignite Your Imagination
Copyright 2018

Why Did the Dinosaurs Die?
Copyright 2019

Winter in Eden
Copyright 2020 – Winner of the 2022 Illumination Book Awards Bronze Medal

The Revelation of Jesus Christ
Copyright 2020

Spiritual Exhaustion
Copyright 2021 - Winner of the 2022 Illumination Book Awards Silver Medal

Forgiving Yourself
Copyright 2021

Lame for Life
Copyright 2022

Quiet ~ A devotional
Copyright 2022

For Hub. Thanks for all the years and all the nonsense.
I love you.

Table of Contents

Personal appearance

Makeup

You would think that after many years of wearing makeup I would have this down pat, but I don't. I have never been able to master eye shadow. Why is it not possible to apply eye shadow evenly to both eyelids? One side always ends up with more on it than the other. Then I have to apply more to the skimpy side, which then ends up with more than the other side. This continues until I look as though I've been in a fight. I then have the choice of appearing in public with two black eyes, or trying to take it off and start again. As I am always pressed for time, I choose the two-black-eyes option. This results in people giving me some strange looks. Since I am tall anyway, with extra-large feet, and usually wearing men's shoes, I suspect some people think I am a man. The fact that I am now sprouting facial hair doesn't help matters.

Then there's mascara. Why won't mascara remain on the eyelashes? It comes off, almost immediately. I have dark circles under my eyes anyway, which I attempt to camouflage with concealer. The concealer seems to encourage the mascara to rub off. So, I can take my pick of black circles under my eyes caused by mascara, or caused by nature. Neither one looks good.

We've all seen People Who Wear Too Much Makeup. Usually these are teenage girls, or old ladies. I used to snicker at the old ladies, until I became one. I now understand their reasoning. If you put more on, eventually the wrinkles and age spots will be completely covered up, right? But at the end of the day, it's sad when three makeup remover wipes have barely made a dent in the archaeological site that is my face. What's that – a birthmark on my cheek? I forgot I had that…

Nails

I have noticed a trend that I can only call "square nails." Women seem to think that getting their nails made into a square shape at a salon is attractive. I don't understand this. What is the purpose of this? No one naturally has square fingernails. I look at it this way: no one tries to make her breasts square…on purpose.

I worry about the future.

The trouble with fake nails is that they are, well, fake. Sometimes a gal needs her nails to open a pop top, remove a staple, scratch an itch, etc. Fake nails are just not durable. The press-on ones have a tendency to fall off if they are used for anything other than display purposes. And the chemical ones are way too thick and hard to maintain. If you have those glue-on kind, you have to keep going back for a "fill-in," and when you finally take them off, your natural nails are basically dead.

But on the plus side, they do come in a dizzying array of colors and patterns.

The salon

Somebody gave me a gift card to a salon, so I decided to go all out. I signed up for a waxing and a mani-pedi. Being a planner, I scheduled this weeks in advance. I am not into Professional Grooming, so this was a new, exciting adventure for me.

On the appointed day, I arrived at the salon all bright-eyed and bushy-tailed. The perky salon gal settled me on the operating table – oops, I mean, the waxing table, and started applying hot wax to my legs. I'll admit, it was kind of soothing. Then she started ripping the wax off my legs.

That wasn't so soothing. But, I was determined to grin and bear it. When she was finished with my legs, she moved on to my underarms. That was even less soothing.

After all the hair had been ripped off my body, my skin was a bright red color. My arms were locked into a permanent "hands-up!" position, because it was too painful to lower them. My legs stuck out stiffly off the edge of the table.

"Okay!" Miss Perky said. "Time for your pedicure!" Unfortunately, this required me to get off of the table go to another room.

I swung my legs off the table and made a valiant effort to stand up. "You can put your arms down now," Miss Perky said.

"Um, no I can't," I said.

"Oh, you jokester!" she giggled. "The pedicure room is right down this hallway." She led the way and I followed, doing my best impression of a wooden soldier. She settled me into the electric chair – oops! I mean, the pedicure chair, and told me that someone would be right with me.

I decided that I really ought to lower my arms. I thought it was best to do this gradually. I finally got them down. Miss Perky had inadvertently left microscopic pieces of wax on my underarms, which caused my arms to then lock into a permanent "down" position.

The pedicure gal entered the room. She was not nearly as perky as Miss Perky. In fact, one could not describe her as perky at all. She was Very Serious. She sat on a little stool in front of the pedicure chair and looked at my legs.

"You seem to have a skin irritation," she observed.

Up until then, I had reminded myself about the "new adventure" aspect of the salon experience.

But at that moment, the adventure began to wear thin.

"I just came from the torture chamber – oops! I mean, the waxing room," I said in a tone of voice that was not adventurous.

"Well, no wonder!" Serious pronounced. "We don't usually do pedis after waxing. You should reschedule."

I took several deep breaths, which inflated my lungs so much that my arms popped off of my sides, where they had been previously held fast by leftover wax. "Ow! No, I'm not going to - ow! reschedule. This was planned weeks in - ow! advance. I told the person who answered the phone what I was having done. If there was a problem, she should have – ow! told me at that time!"

"Well, I guess we can do it," Serious said dubiously.

Just then another person stuck her head in. "How much longer are you going to be in here?" she asked. "We need the room for a bridal party." (At this point we had been in the room for a total of about two minutes.)

Serious was about to answer, but I think she caught a glimpse of my face. She got up and quickly left the room. I could hear a muffled conversation in the hallway. I tried to calm myself by thinking of a tropical beach. In my fantasy, I am lying on the sand, wearing a very fashionable swimsuit. My body is hairless and my mani-pedi is flawless. My husband strolls up to me and hands me a frosty drink, the kind with the little umbrella sticking out of it. I smile up at him. He says, "That's a really nice swimsuit." I bat my eyes, and no mascara comes off.

My fantasy was ruined by the opening of the door and the re-entrance of Ms. Serious. She had another person with her.

"We are going to give you a manicure and a pedicure at the same time!" Serious said. She tried to smile, but I could tell it was a foreign expression for her.

"That's fine," I said calmly. "Whatever works for you."

A small army of salon gals entered the room. One worked on my right foot, one on my left. One grabbed my right hand, another grabbed my left hand. I did not pay attention to what they were doing. I ignored them. I preferred to remain on the tropical beach.

Side note: some women think manicures and pedicures are relaxing. I wonder why?

When it was all over, I walked stiffly out of the salon, wearing the cute paper shoes that they gave me. In the lobby, a group of young women were waiting, all wearing matching t-shirts that said, "Bridal Party." They glared at me.

When I got home, I showed the results to my husband. (I call him Hub to protect his identity.) He surveyed my bright red legs and underarms, my right and left hands, whose nails were painted in two different (although complementary) colors, and my paper shoes.

"What do you think?" I asked. He was silent for a moment, then said, "I'm glad you didn't have to pay for that yourself."

That was on a Friday. The next day, Saturday, less than twenty-four hours after my visit to the salon, the polish came off my right thumbnail, all in one piece. I mean, it just fell off. A perfect, complete thumbnail, made of nail polish, fell off my hand and landed on the floor.

I have come to the conclusion that Professional Grooming is not for me. I am perfectly capable of torturing myself at home.

Hair

I have always had a love/hate relationship with my hair. I love it because I am grateful that I have some. I hate it because it will not obey me.

I have 80's hair. I have no choice. My hair is very thick and very straight. My choices are flat and limp, or big and puffy. I have a thin face, big nose, and pointed chin, so flat and limp makes me look like a crack addict. Since I already have enough problems with the black eyes, dark circles, and facial hair, I choose to go with the Dolly Parton-on-a-bad-day hair. It wouldn't be so bad if I had a Dolly Parton figure to go with the hair, but I don't. I can't even fake her singing voice. I used to dye my hair blond, but then I felt obligated to stuff my bra, and what with always being so pressed for time in the morning, well…it just didn't work out.

I've noticed that the anti-dandruff shampoos give me more dandruff. Why is that? Is this some con job put over by the shampoo industry? The more you shampoo, the more you need to shampoo. Does this make sense? Then I tried conditioning my hair to get rid of some of the 80's look. This backfired. It became puffy *and* greasy, like Dolly after working the fryer at McDonald's.

I really hate having my hair cut. It's a humiliating experience. Those who cut hair for a living must be required to take some sort of vow. This is known as the "Ridicule Current Haircut" vow. It goes something like this:

Haircut Lady: "Who cut your hair last?"
Me: (Actually, several replies are possible here. Depending on my mood, I may answer with any of the following…)
"Callie at Cost Crashers."
"Sallie at Salon Slash."
"Hallie at Hair Haven."
"My mother."
"My sister."
"My husband."
"I just put my head in the ceiling fan last time."

Regardless of my reply, the Haircut Lady will sniff and register her extreme disapproval.
Lady: "Well, it's very uneven."
Me: "That's how I like it."
Lady: (Silence)

At this point she picks up a tiny comb, suitable for combing Barbie's hair, and starts yanking it through my locks. Tears of pain start rolling down my face. I spy a much larger comb.

Me: "Can you use that one? My hair is really thick, and – "
Lady: "This one works better."
Me (silently): "Works better for whom?"

It takes the Haircut Lady a LONG time to get the Barbie comb through my hair. The comb is now broken and missing several teeth. She sniffs disapprovingly again.

Lady: "What kind of conditioner do you use?"
Me: "I don't use conditioner."
Lady: "You don't use conditioner?!?!?! Why not?!?!"
Me: "It makes me look like Dolly at the fryer...never mind."
Lady: "If you used conditioner, it would be a lot easier to comb your hair."
Me: "If you used a normal-sized comb, it would be a lot easier to comb my hair!"
Lady: (More silence)

There are now large, snarled balls of my hair on the floor. It looks like a couple of cats went at it, and at least one didn't survive. Haircut Lady finally starts cutting. She works away in silence, sniffing disapprovingly every once in awhile. When she is finished, I catch a glimpse of myself in the mirror. My mascara has now completely run off of my eyelashes and down my cheeks. This is what happens when Barbie's comb is used on 80's hair.

I finally get to leave the haircut place. A carload of teenage boys drives past. "Dude looks like a lady!" they sing.

I knew I should have worn the other shoes.

***

I've seen a lot of old ladies with black hair. I'm not sure which is worse on someone over the age of seventy, black hair or red hair. Either way, the result is pathetic. Do these women really think they're fooling anyone? Do they stand in front of the mirror and say to themselves, "I'm seventy-two years old, but with my hair dyed black I don't look a day over sixty-nine."

***

I decided to add blond streaks to my hair. I thought this would liven up my "look" a little. I bought the kit at the drugstore and read the directions. How hard could it be?

A couple of hours later, I had inch-wide orange stripes in my hair. Apparently, it was a lot harder than it seemed. I drove back to the drugstore and walked in with my hood up. I found a box of hair color that was close to my God-given shade. I figured that there was probably no way I could un-

18

do the orange stripes, but at least I could cover them up.

"Cold outside?" the clerk asked me, eyeing my hood.

"Uh, yeah, it's really quite unseasonably cold for August," I lied.

A couple of hours later my hair was back to its normal, unlively shade.   I was quite relieved that the orange stripes were now invisible.   I had formulated a contingency plan in case the re-dye job didn't work. I had my black Sharpie ready to go; I figured black stripes in my hair would be slightly more acceptable than orange stripes. Luckily, I didn't have to use it.

Kids

Kids absorb everything, all the time. I learned this when my son was eighteen months old. He was sitting on the living room floor, playing with his blocks, when he slammed one block down on top of another and shouted a new word, very loudly. This was not a word that Hub or I had taught him. It rhymes with truck.

After I regained consciousness, I began to reflect upon where my innocent child could have learned this new word. This required some detective work. I finally traced the origin of his linguistic expansion to some construction workers who had been at his babysitter's house.

This called for a serious consultation with Hub. "We can't let him say that word!" I fretted. "What if we take him out in public and he says it? People will think we are unfit parents!"

Hub fixed me with a steely gaze. "If you ignore it, he will stop saying it," he wisely pronounced.

I had my doubts, but to my surprise, it worked. I ignored it, and Zach didn't say that word again. When he was much older, I recounted the story to him.

"And, you never said it again!" I finished triumphantly. He rolled his eyes.

"Yeah, not in front of you!" he smirked.

Zach is way too much like Hub.

***

Kids will never lie to you, especially about the way you look. This is helpful when needing an honest opinion. Spouses will lie. They don't mean to be dishonest, but they don't want to hurt your feelings. Kids are not concerned about this. For example, I was between haircuts, and after suffering so much at the last salon I put off making another appointment. I was trying to style my hair and becoming increasingly frustrated. I picked up some scissors and started whacking away. My son was alarmed by this. "Mommy, what are you doing?" he asked.

"Well, my hair doesn't look very good, so I'm giving myself a haircut," I replied. This seemed to satisfy him, because he left. After awhile he returned. I was by that time applying makeup. He studied me for awhile.

"Mom," he finally said, "the haircut didn't help."

I really didn't need an honest opinion.

I put this in the same category as what I fondly remember as "the rear episode." I was examining myself in the mirror and muttered something that included the word "fat." Zach overheard this. He shook his head confidently. "Oh, Mommy," he said, "you're not fat. The only part of you that's fat is your butt."

I got a little misty-eyed with pride over that one. He came up with it all by himself.

Being a parent

Nothing really prepares you for being a parent, and the books aren't honest about it. For example, nowhere does anyone tell you that diapers leak. Back in the day, cloth diapers were the only choice, and they leaked. Disposable diapers were supposed to solve that problem. They didn't.

After one particularly bad blow-out, I was sitting on the back seat of the car, changing my newborn's diaper on my lap, and trying desperately to deal with the, um, overflow. I told Hub, tersely, to drive home immediately so I could change clothes. Moms always pack a change of baby clothes in the diaper bag, but funnily enough, I never thought to pack a change of clothes for myself.

As we were driving home, the car was permeated with the odor of "diaper." Since I was covered with it, I didn't notice it so much, but poor Hub was almost overcome. His eyes began to water, and the car started weaving in and out of the lane. "Just try to hold on, honey!" I pleaded. "We're almost home!"

We pulled into the driveway and we both exited the vehicle. Zach was sleeping blissfully in his car seat. Hub draped himself over the roof of the car and took several deep breaths. I decided it was best to take off my clothes in the garage. After a quick sponge-off and fresh clothes, I was as good as new. We did have to stop and buy some car air fresheners…

Motherhood definitely changes a woman. Within a short time of my son's birth, I had been pooped on, peed on, puked on, spit on, vomited on, bled on, and snotted on. And it was all in a day's work.

Men, on the other hand, don't deal with secretions quite as well. One time, Hub had been holding Zach, when he suddenly handed him off to me and ran out of the room. "What's going on?" I demanded.

"I have to change my shirt; he spit up on me," he said queasily.

"Where? I didn't notice him spitting up," I countered.

"Look. Right here." Hub pointed to a microscopic drop of moisture on his sleeve.

Really? For a mom, that shirt would be worn for four more days before finding its way into the laundry.

Something about going through the process of childbirth actually changes the molecular structure of a woman's mind. The brain cells that once connected only with Chanel, Estee Lauder and Macy's now easily connect with every type of nasty bodily fluid, with no problem.

I don't know if that's a good thing....

Animals

I love dogs and cats equally. They each bring their own merits to the table, sometimes literally to the table. My cat will not stay off the table. When I am typing on my laptop, she feels a strong desire to help me type, so she walks helpfully all across the keyboard. Once she managed to press ctrl-alt-delete all at the same time – don't ask me how she did it. This did not bode well for the Important Thing that I was typing.

It wouldn't be so bad if she would just admit her guilt, but she never does. After ruining my brilliant work, she flops down on the keyboard and starts licking various parts of her body. "Oh, am I in your way? Too bad."

When I am eating, she tries to help me by dragging her tail across my plate. If it's something that smells especially yummy, she will tap the edge of my plate with her paw. "Don't forget me, Mom! I'm right here! I'm starving to death! Soon I will be dead, and you'll be sorry!"

Cats are supposed to be so smart, but I have my doubts. My cat will hide under the bed with her tail sticking out. I play along and stand next to the bed, calling her name. It's all fun and games until I tweak her tail. She finds no humor in that.

She is very affectionate, though. Sometimes she will climb onto my chest when I'm in bed, and put her nose on my nose. This is very sweet. Then she begins nibbling my nose, oh, so gently. This is so sweet. Until she decides to chomp down on my nose with the full force of her little cat jaws. Then it stops being sweet and becomes not sweet.

I researched this behavior online. Apparently, in the world of cats, this means, "You belong to me." Thankfully the bleeding stopped eventually.

On the farm we had a lot of cats. My dad was not fond of cats, so naturally they gravitated to him. One morning I was watching him through the window. My brothers were holding the sheep and prying their jaws open so my dad could forcefully insert de-wormer in their mouths. This was quite entertaining. It became even more entertaining when my cat jumped up on a fence post behind my dad. She was very interested in the proceedings. Every once in a while, she would stretch her paw out towards him and wave it in the air. Finally, she decided she'd had enough of that and crouched in the universal "I'm about to launch" cat pose. Without warning, she leaped off the post and onto my dad's back. He stood bolt upright from the bent-over position he had been in, and flung his arms up in the air, waving them wildly. The cat was catapulted off his back and landed somewhere in the sheep pen. The sheep escaped his grasp and began running frantically around the pen. The air was filled with the sound of birds chirping, sheep bleating, a cat yowling, and teenagers laughing their fool heads off. And of course, the new words I learned that day from my dad.

***

Dogs are just as entertaining. I used to have a dog that woke me up every morning by putting his very cold nose in my ear. It never failed. I would sit up in bed screaming, and he would jump up and down excitedly. "Did I wake you? So sorry."

This same dog once caught a mouse. It's true. I was in the kitchen, and I heard quite a commotion coming from the living room. I whipped around in time to see Sarge standing there, with a mouse tail hanging out of his mouth. Horrified, I flung open the back door, and he ran out into the yard. He actually spit the mouse out of his mouth. He stood guard over it, looking uneasily over his shoulder back at me. "Oh, no," I said. "You're on your own." The mouse eventually regained consciousness. I suppose it had experienced a sort of "Jonah in the whale" episode. It made a few attempts to run away, but Sarge used his paw to block it on every side. Finally, it played dead. Sarge poked it a few times, then got bored and came to the door. The mouse saw his opportunity and escaped.

Sarge was a very unusual dog. He loved to eat carrots. It's true. When I brought carrots home from the grocery store, he would whine until I gave him one. He would then lie down and hold the carrot upright between his front paws, and chew it down until it was a nub. I tried to train him to clean up the shredded carrot from the floor, but he never caught on. Dogs can be taught to rescue a drowning person and pull a dog sled, but they cannot be taught to clean ANYTHING. Licking their owners' faces does not count.

***

A baffling incident occurred at my house recently. Something chewed one of my outdoor plants off to the ground. I mean, it looked like it had been mowed off. I stood there looking at it in consternation. Slowly, my gaze shifted to the right. There was a hole in the ground, about two inches in diameter, and one of the (very large) leaves from the plant was sticking out of the hole. I began to put two and two together. Whatever this creature was that had destroyed my plant, it decided to drag the leaves into its underground lair, but was foiled when they were too large to fit into the hole it had dug.

I was torn between revulsion and fascination. What was this creature? What did it look like? I imagined a network of secret underground passages beneath my house, whereby this creature and its friends would travel and meet for secret rendezvous.

Revulsion won out. I raced to the hardware store and bought a big box of mothballs. I stuffed the hole full of them. "Take that, you, you, whatever you are!" I shouted at the hole.

The next day, there was a freshly-dug hole about six inches from the first hole. I stuffed it full of moth balls. The following day, there was another hole, slightly smaller than the first two (getting tired, are you?) nearby. I stuffed it also. After that, the hole-digging ceased. I can only assume they moved the headquarters of their secret society to my neighbor's yard.

Sorry, Bob, but this is war.

Shopping

What is it about women's clothing? Why can't clothing manufacturers get their acts together? I have a skirt hanging in my closet that is a size 4, and it fits, and I wear it. I'm not joking. I also have a size 14 skirt which I wear frequently. It fits nicely. And I have every size in between those two sizes. I wear all of these items, and they all fit. Something is very wrong here. Hub can walk into any store that sells jeans, look at the size on the back, *and buy them without trying them on.* They always fit. There is never any variation in the size of men's clothing. This is terribly unfair. I can try on four different pairs of jeans in four different sizes, and none of them will fit. Then I get so nervous, because I can hear the sales clerk outside the dressing room talking on her little walkie-talkie thing about a "possible shoplifter…too long in the dressing room," etc., and I have to wad all the jeans up and get out as quickly as I can before security arrives.

One day I was more irritated than usual by this, and opened the dressing room door and stuck my head out. "Excuse me? Walkie-talkie lady? Can you come here a minute?" She tried to pretend that she couldn't hear me, but finally came over, eyeing me suspiciously.

"How can I help you?" she asked politely.

31

"Can you bring me some more sizes? I have here sizes 4, 6, 8, and 10, and none of them fit, so could you bring me sizes 5, 7, 9, and 11, please?"

"Those are Junior sizes," she explained as though talking to a five-year old.

"Yes, I know," I smiled sweetly. "You see, since I am a WOMAN, but the women's sizes don't FIT me, I thought I should try reverting back to JUNIORS."

She came back a few minutes later with a size thirteen that fit me perfectly. Go figure.

The size problem is exacerbated by the manufacturers' inexplicable need to keep fiddling with the sizes. Case in point: I have a favorite pair of jeans that I've worn for about fifteen years now. They are size ten and fit perfectly. I recently bought another pair of jeans from the same manufacturer that are size eight, and they fall off of me. I can just pull them on and off without having to unbutton or unzip them. Now, I don't want to embarrass the manufacturer by naming names, but it rhymes with "Teddy Flower."

Why fiddle with the sizes? Why would a size ten fit perfectly and a size eight be too big? Hub says it's supposed to be an ego boost for women. "Look, honey! Ten years ago I wore a size twelve, and now I'm down to a two!" I can see where this is going, and it's not pretty. As in:

Salesperson: "What size are you looking for?"
Me: "Um, I think I wear a negative five this year."

Shopping is just so stressful. There is the size inconsistency issue. Then there is what I call the snootiness issue. I can't help it if I need to buy a bra occasionally. Even middle-aged women with facial hair have to buy bras. It doesn't help that the sale clerks at the lingerie store are all twenty-one and showing their cleavage. None of them are Dolly wannabes, even with the cleavage. Their hair is not big and puffy, but neither is it flat and limp. They wear lots of makeup and none of their mascara rubs off.

I think they must have some kind of regular staff meeting every morning before the mall opens. "Now girls, remember, our target customer is age twenty-two. We do get the occasional frumpy, I mean, mature customer who wanders in by mistake. Just humor her if you can. Always try to spray the newest fragrance directly into her eyes!"

I could teach those twenty-somethings a thing or two. What do they know about nursing a baby while wearing a Body by Victoria bra? It takes practice, but it can be done. If the bra remains unhooked for an hour or so afterward, who would notice? The nursing sweater is so big and bulky it hides everything anyway.

I'm forced to wear men's clothing sometimes, especially shoes. Hub doesn't understand this. He tells me that if he had wanted to marry a man, he would have.

My husband loves shopping. He actually enjoys it. I was born without the female shopping gene, and he got it, and that's okay with me. But, he buys things from the store and then returns them. Frequently. This is a concept I cannot grasp.

Me: "Why did you return those jeans?"
He: "I didn't want them."
Me: "Uh…why did you buy them if you didn't want them?"
He: "Well, duh! I didn't know I didn't want them until after I bought them!"

I've come to the conclusion that I just don't care anymore. What is fashion, anyway? It's just something that rich, skinny people dreamed up to make the rest of us feel bad. If I want to wear a size XL Go-Go's t-shirt out in public, that's my business. I was heartened, though, by an article I read regarding a change in the fashion industry. Some foreign country, I forget which, now requires that its runway models weigh at least 118 pounds. At least, mind you. That really is a comforting thought.

***

Zach and I were in the grocery store, and we saw a four-hundred-pound woman using one of those motorized scooters. Sensing that my son was about to blurt out something that might be tactless, I quickly hustled him to another part of the store. I could tell the scooter had made a bigger impact on him than the size of the woman driving it. "Mom," he finally asked, "can I use one of those things? It would save me the effort of walking." This, at four years old.

Catalogue shopping

I was excited to see in a catalogue that you can actually buy padded underwear. No joke! There are little empty pockets on the buns where you can slip the pads in. I showed Hub the picture. "Look, honey! You can make your butt look bigger! I'm going to order these! My butt's too small – chortle, snort, guffaw!"

My husband, strangely, did not seem to see the humor in this. He fixed me with That Look over the top of his glasses. "That is for certain women who have flat butts. A flat butt is not attractive. It looks like a man's butt. Not a good look." I twisted around to try to see my butt. It is definitely not flat. However, it *does* look like a man's butt. A carload of teenage boys can't be wrong. I am suddenly stricken with self-doubt. Should I buy the padded underwear, or not? Wouldn't that just be an unnecessary expense? Couldn't I just stuff something down there, such as mismatched socks? But how would I prevent them from shifting to unwanted areas? Hmm. Better mull this one over for awhile.

I recently modeled some new pants for Hub. I was excited about my purchase and I was executing little turns in front of the mirror. "What do you think?" I asked. He was silent for awhile. Finally, he said, "Those pants make you look homeless."

By "homeless," I assume he meant carefree and unencumbered. As he was walking away it occurred to me that I may have misheard him. "Did you say 'homeless' or 'hopeless'?" I asked.

Catalogue shopping, like all shopping, is stressful for me. They expect you to take your measurements and order items accordingly. Well, this just isn't realistic. I measure my waist, and carefully write the number down. Immediately, I have a problem. According to the size chart, I am a size six. This is really funny, so I start laughing, but then I stop abruptly. I remember wearing a size six – I know I did. I think I was age six at the time. But still…

The hip measurement causes me more concern. The size chart in the catalogue says I am a size fourteen. So now, all I need to do is flip through the catalogue until I find a garment that is a size six at the waist and a size fourteen at the hip. This shouldn't be so hard…

Okay, so such a garment doesn't exist. I surreptitiously flip to the men's section of the catalogue. I have to do this secretly, without Hub's knowledge. Oh yeah, this is more like it. Lots of nice things to choose from, and cheaper, too. My glee is interrupted. "Are you buying more men's clothes?" he demands. Uh, oh.

"Just looking at gift ideas for you, dear," I say, batting my eyes at him. Batting my eyes causes more mascara to slide off of my lashes. Maybe that will distract him and he will forget about the catalogue. It works. He stares at the black smudges intently, then turns his attention back to his laptop. I have dodged this bullet for now, but for how much longer?

The end result of all this is that I have many clothing items that fit great around the hips, but are far too big around the waist. This is exasperating. One day in frustration I stuffed my son's soccer ball into my skirt waistband. Now it fits beautifully! Off to work I go. A co-worker stares at me. She finally approaches me and gushes, "I didn't know you were pregnant!"

"I'm not pregnant," I smile sweetly. "I'm just conducting a little experiment."

She gapes at me. You would think this was unusual, or something. Some people have no imagination.

Household chores

We seem to generate a lot of garbage, for some reason. My husband and I have very different ideas about garbage. I believe that garbage should go in the garbage can. My husband puts select items in the garbage can, and puts other items in a separate sack, next to the garbage can.

Me: "Why is this empty juice bottle in this sack?"
He: "It took up too much room in the garbage can."
Me: "It's garbage! It belongs in the garbage can!"
He: "It takes up too much room."
Me: "The garbage takes up too much room in the garbage can?!?!?"

This makes it difficult to make a full run, as it were, to the garbage can outside. My philosophy is, you stuff the trash bag as full as you possibly can before taking it out. Hub's philosophy is, the fewer items in the bag at any given time, the better. One time I had just finished taking the garbage out. My son threw his empty juice box and straw in the trash can. I was trying to talk to Hub about some padded underwear I was thinking of buying, or something similar, but I could tell he wasn't listening. He was all nervous and twitchy. I was saying, "…so I think it would really enhance my -" when he cut me off in mid-sentence. "I've got to take the trash out," he said, twitching, and grabbed the empty juice box and bolted out the door. I didn't have the heart to tell him he'd left the straw in the sack. But, when he came back, he took it out and put it in a separate sack next to the empty trash can, so all is good.

Hub and I are both quite squeamish, but thankfully, in different areas. As I mentioned earlier, bodily fluids disgust him. With me, it's things that crawl.

One day Hub came to me, green-faced. He looked like he was about to keel over. I grabbed him and shouted, "Honey, what's wrong?!?"

"There's…there's…a booger in the sink," he said faintly.

Whatever I was expecting, it wasn't that. "A booger? Oh, my. I'd better take care of that." I marched to the sink to have a look. A small glob of dried liquid soap had fallen off the end of the dispenser, and was lying serenely in the bottom of the sink. I quickly washed it down the drain, then went to find Hub.

He was lying on the couch with a cool cloth on his forehead, eyes closed. "Hub?" I whispered in his ear.

"No, no…." he moaned.

"Hub, listen to me," I said firmly. "It was soap. Just soap. Not a booger. Soap."

"Soap?" His eyes slowly opened. "Are you sure?"

"Quite sure," I smiled at him. "Everything is fine now."

He seemed to snap out of it suddenly. "Of course, everything's fine. Why wouldn't it be?" He got up off the couch and walked off.

Now, lest you think otherwise, the division of labor in our household is really quite fair. A few days later, I ran out of the house, into the garage, screaming. "What's wrong?!?" Hub demanded.

"There's a spider on the ceiling!" I screamed.

"A spider? What kind of spider?" he asked.

"How should I know what kind of spider? It's big and black and ugly! Kill it! Kill it!" I ran out of the garage, into the street, screaming, "Kill it! Kill it!" I don't know what the neighbors thought…

A few minutes later Hub found me, and led me gently back into the house. He assured me that the spider was dead. I seemed to snap out of it suddenly. "Of course, the spider is dead. It's really no big deal." The open umbrella over my side of the bed is just there for decoration, really.

I cannot think of one place where creepy-crawly critters are welcome, not even the zoo. Now, someone is going to get all offended and tell me that birds eat insects, so they serve a useful purpose in the food chain and in the circle of life, blah, blah blah. I don't buy it. Birds can eat seeds. There is no reason for bugs, spiders, snakes, or anything that has more than four legs to exist. That's my story and I'm sticking to it.

Telemarketers

My last name is Turkish. It's hard for a lot of people to pronounce. It's good though, because I can immediately identify the telemarketers. I like to have fun with these people.

Me: "Hello?"
Telemarketer: "Good evening, Mrs. (long pause) Onhonser...?"
Me (sweetly): "I'm sorry, there's no one here by that name."
Telemarketer: "Oh, I apologize. I can certainly speak to you, ma'am – "
Me: (more sweetly) "No, you certainly can't (click)."

We're on a telemarketing do-not-call list, but they call anyway. It doesn't help. Why don't telemarketers sell something that people would actually want? For example:

Telemarketer: "Ma'am, I'd like to tell you about our new product line. We offer women's fashions for the uniquely-shaped female. All of our clothing has a size six waist, while offering a size fourteen hip. You can't pass this opportunity by!"
Me: "No, I can't! Please ship a dozen ASAP!"
Telemarketer: "We also offer underwear with these little pockets where you can slip some padding in – "

Me: "Yes, yes, yes!"
Telemarketer: "And size eleven shoes – "
Me: "Some of each color, please! And hurry!"

Well, the UPS man came today. I plan to wear the underwear with the little pads in it tonight. We'll see if Hub notices.

School

My son attends a private school. We all like it, but you know, I thought I had finished with school long ago. It's hard to get back in the groove, so to speak. And school has changed so much since I went. They call this "parental involvement." We didn't have "parental involvement" when I went to school.

I read a notice sent home from my son's teacher. "We are currently studying the letter R in class. Please remember to send something to school tomorrow with your child that begins with the letter R." As if I didn't have enough to worry about. I cast my eyes around my kitchen. R, R, R. Rice-a-Roni begins with R. I wonder if it matters if it's already cooked? I wish the teacher would have been a little more specific. Rigatoni begins with R, but we don't have any. Refuse? We sure have a lot of that. I eye the Refrigerator for awhile, then discard that idea. I ferret a rubber band out of the junk drawer. Rubber band begins with R. This should work. I call Zach to my side and show him the rubber band. "I'm putting this in your back pack. You need to give it to your teacher tomorrow." His eyes light up like a neon sign.

"I can snap Isaiah with this, Mommy! He won't be able to snap me back because he won't have one! Ha, ha! I'll get him good!" He snaps me on the leg a few times for practice.

"Ow! No, the rubber band isn't for snapping people. You need to give it to your teacher. You're studying the letter R, and rubber band begins with R."

I got another notice sent home from the teacher that evening. "This is a reminder to all parents regarding our zero-tolerance weapons policy. Weapons include, but are not limited to, firearms, knives, pepper spray, etc." After the word "etc." someone had scrawled in "rubber bands". There was another notice with it. "Effective immediately, we are discontinuing our study of the letters of the alphabet until further notice."

Somehow, I don't think we're getting our money's worth.

Exercise

I exercise every morning. Really. We have a weight machine and a treadmill in our basement. This is something fairly new. I used to get up early and go to the gym. This caused a lot of problems. There was always a strange woman in the locker room. When I say strange, I mean she was naked. All the time. You can expect nakedness in a locker room some of the time, but all of the time? No. She always gravitated to me, for some reason.

"Have you tried the shower today? I think it's broken." She said this while standing very close to me, her little, upturned face fixed on my two black eyes. I tried to answer her question without looking at her, which was hard to do.

"Well, no, I haven't tried it. I don't usually shower here, because I don't like people to see me naked..." I don't think she took the hint.

"Well, somebody needs to tell management. They need to get that thing fixed." She sat down, naked, on a bench, just waiting. For what, I don't know. Maybe for maintenance to fix the shower. When I left, she was still sitting there, still naked.

Once in the weight room she approached me, once again standing too close. "Have you tried this machine? I think it's broken." Sweat had run into my eyes, with the dual result of blinding me and intensifying the Million-Dollar-Baby look.

"No, I haven't tried it yet today, I – oh, it's you! I didn't recognize you with your clothes on!"

It was shortly after that when we got our exercise equipment at home. I really like it, but sometimes, I don't know, I just miss the little naked woman. I can't explain it.

Before the gym with the naked woman, I went to a gym that was filled with Very Muscular Men. Being single at the time, this should have been a golden opportunity for me. However, I learned that Very Muscular Men do not look at women in the gym. They only look at their Very Muscular Muscles, in the mirror, from all angles. They flex one muscle, rotate north, south, east and west, then flex the next muscle, and so on. It seems to me that this would get tedious after a while, but no. They can do it for *hours*.

Exercise seems to get harder the older I get. Why is this? If you've been exercising for a long time, shouldn't it keep getting easier? My treadmill has a "recommendation" posted on it. "For best results, do not hold the handgrips while using the treadmill." This is baffling to me. Why are they there, then? What purpose do they serve?

I tried not holding the handgrips. I did not achieve best results. In fact, I fell off the treadmill. But maybe I'm looking at this all wrong. Maybe falling off the treadmill burns more calories than staying on. This can only be a positive thing.

They say you're supposed to drink a lot of water while exercising. My treadmill has a little place to put your water bottle, just for this purpose. But drinking it requires letting go of one of the handgrips for a little while. This is a risky proposition at best. It's okay if a little water spills on the treadmill, isn't it? I've been meaning to clean it anyway…

This is all in keeping with my new resolution, which is to be positive at all times. If life hands you lemons, make lemonade, and all that sort of thing. People really get too uptight over all sorts of unimportant things. Just the other day I was noticing that I wasn't using the proper form while lifting weights on my weight machine. This was according to the little poster on the wall that came with the machine. Now, I could respond to this in two ways. I could get all worked up over the fact that my back wasn't exactly straight, or I could throw my water bottle at the perky little blond on the poster, with a size six waist AND hips. I mean, really, the choice is mine.

I have come to the conclusion that I am very accident-prone. Falling off the treadmill clued me in. Then the other day, I cut myself with a butter knife. Really. I am the only person in the world who has cut herself with a butter knife. I actually needed a band-aid. It really made me stop to think. If a butter knife is intended to spread butter, why is it sharp? Okay, so I realize most people would not describe a butter knife as sharp, but after my finger trauma, I would. A butter knife should just be a flat object with no sharpness to it at all. Similar to a flat chopstick. That would work.

Fitness

I was really irritated when I discovered that I had gained a few pounds. I decided to join one of those online weight-loss programs. I don't want to embarrass them by naming them, so I will refer to them as "Fate Dodgers." I eagerly paid my first month's dues, and awaited the personalized phone call from my personal coach. In the meantime, I began calculating the points of the food I was eating. Prior to my becoming a member, I'd had no idea that food had points. I vaguely thought that points had something to do with sporting events. But no, food has points too.

I quickly discovered that assigning points to food was a complex and baffling undertaking. Quite frankly, the program made no sense to me. By ten a.m., I had used up all the points assigned to me for the day. This paralyzed me. Now what? Do I eat tomorrow's points today? Can I buy more points? Can I borrow a friend's points?

I learned that Fate Dodgers considers multiple foods to have "zero points." So, theoretically, you can eat as many zero-point foods as you want. This also baffled me. I would finish eating all my "pointed foods" – not that they had a pointed shape, but you know what I mean - and then I would start in on the "non-pointed foods." The trouble is, no matter how many non-pointed foods I ate, I was still hungry.

I am not sure who came up with this point system. To make it even more complicated, they assign colors to various divisions within their program. I had to take an online test to discover that I was blue. Well, duh!

I don't think I really thought this whole thing through. How can I say this politely? The people that I've known over the years who have been members of Fate Dodgers, don't look as though they are members of a weight loss group. They look as though they are members of Donuts Unlimited. That should have been my first clue that something was amiss.

Sports

I don't understand sports at all. My sister knows all about sports. She is the coordinated one in the family. Everything on her body is the same size, including her feet. I think it is size three. Anyway, she is a volleyball champion. She can smack that volleyball over the net and behead someone on the other side. She is *dedicated.* She once split her shin open while playing volleyball, and kept playing. With her shin bone exposed. I don't understand this. When I fell off the treadmill I had to go lie down with a cool cloth on my head.

I do have a theory, though, about her athletic ability. I think her feet are so small, that when she jumps she is able to "catch air" more than someone with size eleven feet. Or maybe the phrase is "hang time." I can't remember these sports terms.

My husband likes sports, too. He has tried to explain them to me. I kind of understand figure skating, but...

There is some kind of conspiracy with the cable and satellite companies as to which sporting events they will show, and how they will show them. Once we saw a football game with no sound. Hub had to turn on the radio and listen to the radio broadcast while watching the silent game on TV. This didn't work out very well. The radio broadcast was about five seconds ahead of the picture on the TV. But, on the plus side, he got to know about everything before it happened, so to speak. Like God. I think he kind of had a swelled head after that.

My dad was always watching some sporting event on TV. I say "watching" rather loosely, because he was usually asleep in front of the TV. The moment I would change the channel to something good, like "The Brady Bunch," he would immediately wake up and start hollering. "Turn that back! I was watching it!"

Sleeping through a sporting event is the only way I can endure a sporting event. My dad had the right idea, without even knowing it.

Kids' sports

There are many unwritten rules associated with kids' sports. I didn't know this until I enrolled my son in a few things. I didn't know that the soccer fields each had a name, such as Field A, Field B, etc. In our town there are no signs showing the field names, but each team is supposed to appear on a certain field at a certain time to play. This was difficult for our family. We had to find Field D. We didn't know where it was. The other parents seemed to know, because they were all there. Not only were they there, but they were seated in the proper area. There is an unwritten rule about this, too. I didn't know the parents of the Cougars are not supposed to sit with the parents of the Bears. This was not explained in advance. Unwritten rules are like that. That's why they're called Unwritten Rules.

Anyway, while we were trying to find Field D, I flagged down a lady that looked like she might possibly work at the concession stand. "Do you know where Field D is?" I asked her. "Oh, yes," she said enthusiastically. "Field D is right over there, next to Field 9." This confused me. "Field D is next to Field 9?" I repeated. "Are there any kind of signs labeling them?" "Oh, no, honey," she said, less enthusiastic now. "But they all do go in order, if that helps."

Order? What kind of order is that? Whose order? The definition of order seems to have changed since I was in school.

Kids who are lucky enough to be born with a last name beginning with the letter "A" are always first. My son was always first. Kids line up in "order," and everyone understands this. Now, they want to give kids the opportunity to experience being first, even if their last name is Zimmerman. I have no problem with that. One day Zach's coach told the team to line up in "reverse order by name." Zach, being the brilliant person that he is, went to the first spot in line. His coach reminded him that he needed to go to the last spot in line. He fixed her with a stern look and said, "You didn't specify first or last name."

This incident was recorded on his report card, along with the notation that few first-graders use the word "specify" on any given day.

Old age

I don't consider myself old, really I don't. It's just that certain things seem to irritate me more than they used to. For example, there was a bit of a scandal a few years back over photos of a young celebrity mother out on the town with her friends, just having a good old time, wearing a really short skirt, getting in and out of her limo…well, I just wanted to take her aside and have, you know, a little chat with her.

Me: "Barbie, dear, did your maid forget to do the laundry today?"
Barbie: "What do you mean?"
Me: "Just wondering where your underwear was, dear, that's all."

Back in my day, we always wore underwear. Even on special occasions. There just never was a time when underwear wasn't worn. Now, of course, things are different, I guess. Have to keep up with the times.

I've noticed a few other things, too. Back when, if people were chubby, portly, overweight, not slender (you get the idea), there was this unwritten code about Certain Items That Should Not Be Worn. Now, when I'm at the swimming pool, I see chubby people Wearing Certain Items. At least, I think they are. Sometimes there is so much overlap the Item itself is obscured. This worries me. On the one hand, I think, what if it falls off when they go down the slide? But on the other hand, I think, if it did, who would notice? That is the advantage of having overlap. I guess, the only advantage.

Old people also sometimes wear Certain Items that they would be better off not wearing. For example, an elderly woman came into my office one day, wearing a Winnie the Pooh sweatshirt. Perhaps her granddaughter gave it to her for her birthday, and she felt obligated to wear it. But clothing with cute cartoon characters on it is best left to the preschoolers, in my opinion.

This lady also had black hair, if that tells you anything about her.

Romance

Romance is high on my list. Hub and I really enjoy hugging. Our son's job is to prevent this from happening, any way he can. When Hub and I are hugging, Zach will stop whatever he's doing and insert himself in between us. "You're the bread and I'm the cheese!" he says gleefully. At first this was kind of cute, really endearing. Now, not so much. We have been forced to come up with ingenious ways to hug on the sly, so to speak.

One day, I peeked in Zach's room, and he was busy building something with Legos. Hub was asleep in the recliner. *"Now's my chance!"* I thought. I tiptoed into the living room and silently climbed into the recliner next to Hub. I threw my arms around him and hugged him for dear life.

"What's going on?" he woke up, shouting. "What time is it? Who are you?" This attracted Zach's attention. He came racing into the room, saw us in the recliner, and launched himself into it at full tilt. The recliner and the three of us went over backwards. Zach thought this was hilarious fun.

"Let's do that again!" he yelled. "That was so awesome!"

Hub was also yelling. Did I mention that Hub does not like to be awakened suddenly?

Thankfully, the words he yelled on that occasion were words that Zach had heard before.

I decided it was best to temporarily shelve the "recliner hug."

But I do have high hopes for the padded underwear.

Family

My folks have been married for over fifty years. I have a tremendous amount of admiration for them. Like a lot of long-married couples, they have developed their own set of quirks. They are both hard of hearing, but they are used to it, I guess. A typical exchange between them goes something like this:

Mom: "Quit picking on me!"
Dad: "I am not kicking you!"

They like to sit on the back patio, each with a fly swatter in hand, and swat flies. This would be okay, except they also swat the flies that land on each other. I'm not sure, but they seem to get a lot of enjoyment out of whacking away on each other. I asked Hub about this.

"If a fly landed on me, would you hit me with a fly swatter?" He seemed to take an inordinate amount of time to think about this. Finally, he asked,

"Is a fly swatter my only choice?"

It took me two days to figure out what he meant.

Now that my parents are older, we've all had to make a few adjustments. Mom is in the early stages of dementia, which is hard to deal with.

But, believe it or not, it has its advantages, too. I gave her the first draft of this book to read. I was anxious for her opinion. She called me the next day.

"What is this manuscript you left here for me?" she asked. "It portrays me in an unflattering way! As if I would ever hit Dad with a fly swatter! If I was going to hit him, I would use something much sturdier! I want you to take that part out!" I assured her that I would (not in a million years), and hung up, thinking all was resolved. She called me the next day.

"What is this manuscript you left here for me?" she began. My mind began to wander. I wasn't sure, but I thought I was beginning to detect a pattern. I promised again to do some editing, then slipped back to her house and got rid of the evidence.

I think she will be pleasantly surprised when she reads the final draft.

In Mom's defense, she's always been a little, well, unique. That's where I get it from. Meal preparation at her house is always fraught with uncertainty. I will be rummaging around in the fridge, and she'll say, "Get me the leftover gravy." I'll continue rummaging, trying to identify the gravy. "It's in the container labeled 'ham and beans,' she'll tell me helpfully. Of course! Ham and beans! I'll hand it to her. "Your dad would like a brownie, I'll bet. Those are in the freezer, in a container labeled 'beet juice'."

I always have many questions when I leave Mom's house, such as, why would anyone save beet juice?

(Mom, I love you so much. You have always said that when your time comes, you want to be cremated. I want you to know that I will proudly display your ashes on my mantle, in a yogurt container, with the word "yogurt" crossed out with a black marker, and "cinnamon sugar" written there instead.)

Mom is very, very thrifty. That's where I get it from. She would go to the Bakery Bargain Barn and fill the back of the station wagon with expired bread, cupcakes, apple pies, and sundry items that only the Bakery Bargain Barn had. Then she would haul it all home and we would eat it over the next few weeks. Expired bread really isn't so bad. But the powdered milk she made us drink - *shudder*.

When I was a kid, my mom was really into sewing. I would see the cutest top ever in the store window and beg her to buy it for me. She would say, "I can make that for half the price." After a few times of hearing this, I always began to panic. But

I never learned my lesson. "Mom! Look at that top! Can I get it? Oops! I mean, I don't really want it!" But it was too late. She would be dragging me to the fabric section by then. "Now, you pick out the material you want, while I go look at patterns." The material I wanted was on the shirt in the window. It did not exist anywhere in the yards and yards of fabric bolts in the store. Worse, the pattern she picked out was nowhere near the style of the shirt in the window, either. It took me a long time to catch on to the fact that Mom didn't want me to have the shirt in the window, due to its being too hip and too cool for someone my age. She wanted me to have the cute, darling shirt shown in Simplicity pattern number 8235, which was very retro, very 50's, very frumpy. My closet was filled with those. At least at that age I *could* have worn the cool stuff. That was back before my body acquired its odd shape. Now I'm forced to go with the frumpy stuff. I mourn my lost childhood and what could have been.

My mom is just way too talented with the sewing machine and needles in general. I've tried. I always end up pushing the needle through my finger, or sewing the bottom of the skirt shut, which makes it really hard to put on, or not matching the striped pattern correctly at the seams, which makes the garment look as though it is meant to be worn in the circus, rather than on the street. But the circus look was very popular a few years back…

Come to think of it, both Mom and Dad are handy with needles. Anytime one of us had a splinter or thorn, out came the needle. The anticipation of the needle was always much worse than the actual experience of the needle. I think it was mainly the fact that they were just so darned eager to start poking us with sharp pieces of metal. It would have been okay if they could have just got the thorn out in one try. But it usually involved digging, and digging, and digging.

This is why I don't have a tattoo. Or pierced ears. Or any holes in my body whatsoever, other than the ones I was born with.

***

My dad took a lot of naps when we were kids. Basically, if he wasn't working, he was sleeping. We thought it would be hilariously funny to play a little trick on him while he slept. One of us got an Oreo cookie, and one of us slipped it into his wide-open mouth as he slept. We started giggling and elbowing each other.

"What do you think he'll do when he wakes up and finds a cookie in his mouth?" we snickered. "Maybe he won't notice!" we giggled.

Of course, Dad eventually woke up.   He sat up and started chewing. He had the cookie about half-eaten before he realized that he had not had a cookie in his mouth when he fell asleep. Then a WHOLE BUNCH of new words were learned by us all. These words were quite spectacular in their descriptiveness.

It was fun, but we didn't do it again.

Intelligence

My husband is an engineer. He is Really Smart. He was studying for an engineering exam once, and he had a book called *1001 Problems*. That was actually the name of the book. I'm looking at this book thinking, I have enough problems already, so, no thanks. But Hub could solve all the problems in the book. I'm thinking, if he can solve all those, I'm going to let him have a crack at mine. I talked to him about it. He said when the exam was over, he would see what he could do.

I'm intelligent too, only in a different way. I can't solve *1001 Problems*. I flipped through the book, and I can say with confidence that I can't solve *1 Problem*. But I am really good at other things. How many people do you know who can put together a wardrobe of size six waist and size fourteen hip items? Okay, so I'm still working on that, but still…

I, being a very nerdy person, can read any sentence or paragraph and immediately identify all the spelling errors and grammatical mistakes. Hub, on the other hand, can drive down any street and identify every roof and every wall that is not built on a correct geometrical plane.

"Look at that!" he pointed as we were driving down the street one day. "That's terrible."

I looked. The house had a sign in the yard that said: "GRGJE SALE."

"Oh, wow, that's pathetic," I shook my head. "How could somebody be so ignorant?"

"I don't know," Hub said. He was very indignant. "There's no way that could pass city code."

I smiled at my husband indulgently. "Now, honey," I said. "The sign is ridiculous, I agree, but I don't think the city cares about spelling errors."

"What sign?" he said blankly. "I was talking about the soffit vents. They weren't placed at the proper distance from the roof."

"What's a soffit vent?" I asked.

An hour later, I finally had a vague idea.

That is the difference between an engineer and an English nerd.

007

I think Hub is too smart for his own good. It is my secret belief that he is employed by the government in some hush-hush capacity. I started to get suspicious years ago when we were having a conversation about birth certificates.

"I don't have one," he said casually, as if he could sneak that by me without my noticing.

"Well, you can get one easily," I said. "All you have to do is bring your driver's license to the Records Department –"

"No," he said, "I've never had one. The country I was born in doesn't issue them."

This sounded highly suspicious to me. *The country I was born in doesn't issue them.* "Then you need to write to the Consulate in Beirut – "

"I wasn't born in Beirut. I was born in Athens."

"Then why does your passport say 'Birthplace: Lebanon'?" I demanded. He didn't answer, but suddenly looked uncomfortable. I smelled a rat. I went and dug his passport out and started examining it. "Why is your middle name on your passport different from the one on your driver's license? And why are your parents' names different?"

Like the swirling pieces of a Middle Eastern kaleidoscope, my husband's life as a potential international spy began to take shape in my mind. I suddenly looked at him with fresh eyes.

"You talk to your family members in Arabic," I said accusingly. "You eat falafels. Falafels are tasteless. Why would anyone willingly eat falafels? You drink Turkish coffee! You - "

He left the room, muttering in Arabic. He came back a few minutes later with something in his hand.

"Look, honey!" he said. "A new catalogue came today with men's clothes in it!"

He thinks he can distract me, but I'm not falling for it. At least, I can just peek at the catalogue, and get back to the passport later....

The workplace

I had a boss once that I couldn't understand. I mean I had *no idea* what he meant when he talked to me. E-mails were even worse. He would type every third or fourth word in the e-mail in all caps. If he was really stressed, he'd do every other word. I think this was supposed to be for EMPHASIS.

Me: "How often should we pay the new sub-contractor?"
Boss: "Pay her EVERY two weeks WHEN she is DONE."
Me: "Uh, do you mean pay her every two weeks, or pay her when she is done?"
Boss: "PAY for sub-contractors IS to be on AN individual BASIS. In ACCORDANCE with our cash FLOW policy and payroll CYCLE, SUB-contractors are to be PAID every TWO weeks when THEY are DONE."
Me: "Uhhhhh, do I pay her this Friday or not?"
Boss: "THE cycle OF the SUB-contractor IS to BE aligned WITH the PAY cycle AND the CYCLE of THE project BEING worked ON."
Me: "How about if you pay her?"

Another boss I had I was actually able to understand, but, bless his heart, he was getting up in years. He tried to stay on top of current trends and phrases, but always seemed to be just a little off. One day he asked me to call our credit card company and have them investigate some suspicious transactions. "We must be very careful of personality theft," he reminded me.

Dude, you know I love ya and all, but, I'm pretty sure no one wants your personality.

I've noticed there are a lot of unwritten rules in the workplace. This disturbs me. If they are unwritten, they are bound to be broken sooner or later. This is why I believe all rules are to be written. But as I was compiling my list, I realized this may be impractical.

Rules that should be written for the office

Do not gasp loudly while on the phone.
Do not display in your cubicle sculptures of animals mating.
Do not bring snakes to the office.
Do not come to the office naked.
Do not talk about your gynecological exam in the office.
Unless it is part of your job description, do not set anything on fire in the office.
Do not eat more than twelve donuts in one day.
If you are too big to fit in a standard office chair, retire (see rule immediately above).

Job interviews are like that, too. Many unwritten rules. I personally love the strengths and weaknesses one.

"Suppose you tell me about your strengths and weaknesses," the interviewer will ask.

What do they really expect you to say?

"Well," I say, my eyes modestly cast down, "when I was a kid, I was really good at blaming my sister for things that I had done wrong. I really believe this skill can transfer over to the workplace. In fact, if anything goes wrong on the job, I can assure you that it will be someone else's fault, not mine."

"Um, that's not exactly what – "

"And as far as weaknesses go," I interrupt, "I've always seemed to have a lot of trouble with my hair. It's either too puffy, or too greasy, or –"

"We'll come back to that later. Tell me about yourself and what you can bring to this job."

"I never eat more than twelve donuts in one day. This requires a tremendous amount of discipline, and in this day and age, with so many undisciplined people in the workplace, I know this will be a huge asset to your company."

I always make eye contact when I say that. Interviewers love eye contact.

There is also the unwritten rule of the parking lot. I have worked at the same job for twelve years, and I have parked in the same spot for twelve years. This all changed when a new person was hired. She parked in My Spot.

At first, I thought this was a fluke and I decided to let it go, even though it made me very nervous. But the next day she did it again. And the day after that, she did it again.

I was faced with a dilemma I had never encountered before. Could I approach her and tell her not to park there, citing legal precedent? I could, but I didn't think that would stand up in court. Could I make a temporary sign that read, "Reserved for employee of the week?" I could, but what if the real employee of the week parked there? Then I would have two interlopers to deal with.

I finally decided I had no other choice than to beat her to it. This was not easy. It required careful planning on my part. My new morning routine went like this: get up, get dressed, throw the makeup in the bag, throw the breakfast and the lunch in the bag, throw the car in reverse and squeal out of the driveway, race to work, and slide into the parking space approximately four minutes before she arrived. I then had a leisurely forty minutes to put on my makeup in the rearview mirror, eat my breakfast, read, do sit-ups, file my nails into a square shape, etc., before I had to be at my desk.

This went on until she finally took a job elsewhere. And that's the problem with unwritten rules. You can't tell someone she's broken an unwritten rule, because it's unwritten, and she won't understand.

Other people's music

From where I sit in my office, I can hear three different radios tuned to three different radio stations. This is not a pleasant experience. One station is top forty hits, one is country, and one is an unidentifiable jumble of shrieks, wails, and metal scraping against glass. I have tried to adapt to this. I realized I was not successful when I typed in the subject line of an email: "It's a quarter after one, and I'm a little drunk…" Unfortunately, I did not realize this until after I had pressed send.

I like to think that my brain requires more concentration than others' brains. Even back in high school, my friends would strew their homework all over the bed, then crank up the radio and start working. I tried to join in on this a few times. At my friend's house one day, I was working dutifully on my social studies assignment. The radio was blasting, my friend was complaining about her boyfriend, and we were supposed to be doing homework at the same time. At one point she asked me, "Can I see your notebook? I'm really stuck on this assignment." She read a few paragraphs, frowning. "This doesn't make any sense. Under "Branches of Government" you wrote "Girls just want to have fun," and under "Checks and Balances" you wrote "Who's going to drive you home tonight?" What the heck is that supposed to mean?

I reminded her that it was very noisy in her bedroom, and suggested politely that maybe we could do our homework in silence for a while? She rolled her eyes. "How are we supposed to concentrate without music?"

I like music as much as the next person, really, I do. I just don't like other people's music. I also am rather old-fashioned. I believe music should be listened to and appreciated for its own merits, not used as background noise for anything.

Why is background noise needed? It makes no sense to me. Case in point: I volunteered to be the cleaning lady for my church. Another nice lady offered to help me. We showed up at the appointed time and started cleaning. She said, "We need some music." I thought, *"Why?"* She turned on her phone. I turned on the vacuum cleaner. She finally found the music she wanted on her phone, and put it on a table "where we can both hear it." Trouble was, I couldn't hear it. All I could hear was the vacuum cleaner. After I had vacuumed the entire sanctuary, which was the last thing I had to do, I was done and ready to go home. I had not heard one note of the music that had been playing "in the background," and did not comprehend its purpose.

I've talked to various people about this, trying to understand. "Music relaxes you," I was told. Now, that statement is dubious. I can assure you, the shrieks, wails, and metal scraping on glass music that I am subjected to at work does not relax me. In fact, I need to listen to music at home in order to relax from the music I was forced to listen to at work.

Some music is relaxing, sure. That stuff they play in Hobby Lobby is unbelievably relaxing. Now contrast that with the stuff they play in those teeny-bopper clothing stores.

Perhaps this is a generational thing that I just don't understand. But I doubt it. I think it's simply that I was born without the "appreciate other people's music" gene, and other people got it, and that's okay with me.

Travel

Oh, how I love to travel. The sights, the sounds, the people, all so new and exciting, and yet so curiously the same as home. I was in a mall in a strange city and saw one of those mall haircut places advertising really cheap cuts. Well, there was no way I could pass that by. But this time, I was prepared! I slid into the chair.

Haircut Lady: "Who cut your hair last time?"
Me: "You did!"

She was speechless. She couldn't even sniff disapprovingly. I really think I sent her into a state of shock. I was even able to remove the Barbie comb from her hand and replace it with a normal-sized one, and she didn't flinch.

Different foods, too, are great to try when you're traveling. It's always just a little disappointing, though, when reality doesn't quite match fantasy. I was in Hawaii and eager to try authentic Hawaiian food. I asked one of locals what would qualify. "Spam," he replied.

"Excuse me?" I asked.

"Spam is the official, authentic food of Hawaii," he said.

He wasn't kidding. Apparently, it was introduced during the war and became wildly popular. Everybody eats it and everybody loves it. Me, not so much. I was hoping for something a little more, I don't know, *tropical*. Spam reminded me way too much of my childhood on the farm.

Mom: "We're having leftover Spam tonight. Can you get it out of the fridge? It's in the container labeled 'cranberries'."

We were traveling in Florida, and stumbled across a cute little seaside restaurant called "Fishette." For some reason, this cracked us up. Is a Fishette a really small fish? Or is it a cute female fish? It became even more hilarious when Hub nicknamed it "Fish Head."

"Where are we eating tonight?"

"FISH HEAD!" Hysterical laughter from me, Hub, and Zach.

Of course, travel is made much easier nowadays with this thing called GPS. But what they don't tell you is how many accidents are caused by people fiddling with their GPS. In the good old days, you simply opened the road map and spread it across your lap, across the lap of the person sitting next to you, across the back seat, out of the windows on both sides of the car, and then you simply looked at the map, looked at the road, looked at the map again, looked at the road again – oops! Wasn't that the exit you were supposed to take? Can't tell; the map was blocking the windshield…

People try to give me directions. While I usually always know what direction I'm going, such as north, south, east, or west, I rarely am able to understand spoken directions. As in:

"Take Highway 2 East and go for about two miles. Take the second right after the light, then turn into the driveway marked by the mailbox with the pink pig on it. You can't miss it."

See, I always get suspicious when they say you can't miss it. I happen to be an expert on missing it. If there is any possible way to miss it, I can.

Once I was traveling in Paris and I stopped to ask a harmless-looking man how to get to the train station. I know he understood me, because he immediately rattled off a very long list of directions, complete with hand gestures. Unfortunately, his directions were in French. I don't speak French. I'm even unsure about the word "oui." I think it means "yes," but it may possibly mean "ouch," or "mailbox with pink pig." Maybe that last one is actually "oui, oui." Anyway, I nodded several times while he was speaking, then ambled off in the direction that he had been vigorously pointing. I actually did arrive at the train station. I think this is because I found a different person who spoke English who told me how to get there.

My ethnic background is Czechoslovakian. I know one phrase in Czech, which is "Já ti dám facku." If I remember correctly, this translates to: "I will slap your face." This is certainly a helpful phrase to know when traveling in the Czech Republic, and I hope to test it out some day.

***

I have a very dear friend for whom English is her second language. Her English is flawless, but it is the little quirks of the language that sometimes don't quite come out right.

One day she asked me, "What is that thing called – you know, that thing that they throw on the ground when they are finished smoking?"

I said, "Oh, a cigarette butt?"

She nodded vigorously. "Yes, that's it. And they are so careless with it! They start fires! They just carelessly throw that thing down, that cigarette bun, and a fire starts!"

My mind immediately latched onto the term "cigarette bun." Cigarette bun sounds like a horrible accident that occurred at the bakery.

Today only! Cigarette buns 75% off!

My dad also grew up speaking a native language - Czech - other than English. He, too, spoke flawless English, but had a bad habit of substituting random words for the correct word that he couldn't think of at the time.

Once, he gave me a key chain with a clip on it. "Here," he said, "clip that to your cleat."

"Excuse me?" I asked. I was not aware that I had a cleat. I was not sure what it was, or where it was located, even.

"Right there," he pointed to my belt. "Clip it there."

"My belt?" I asked. "Okay, that I understand."

We all got a lot of enjoyment out of my dad's verbal slips. If we were making too much noise, he would yell, "Be quiet! The news are on!" One time he mixed up the words "immorality" and "immortality," with hilarious results. My imagination went wild with that one.

"And now, dearly beloved, we are gathered here today to celebrate our sister's life. She has now crossed over into immorality."

Depending on the audience, that statement could be either a crowd-pleaser or a riot-inciter. Or, possibly both.

Food

Who doesn't love food? Food is a wonderful invention. I love to watch those cooking shows on TV, the kind where the contestants get three ingredients, such as red-hots, squid, and potato peelings, and have to make a gourmet meal out of them.

There is always so much drama on these shows. Someone always starts crying, someone stomps off the set, someone else throws a knife at another contestant; it's always something.

I have never been invited to be on any of these shows, probably because my method of cooking is too simple. My philosophy is this: try to make the food taste somewhat like God intended it to taste. Those who are gourmet cooks have an opposite philosophy: try to make the food taste absolutely unrecognizable as to what it originally tasted like before they started tinkering with it.

Case in point: I was in an upscale restaurant with my friend, celebrating my birthday. We ordered roasted Brussels sprouts as an appetizer. I thought something was up when they came out, drenched in some kind of brown sauce. I bravely took a bite. Turns out the brown sauce was melted brown sugar.

"Are you okay?" my friend asked, concerned.

"I'm…going…into…diabetic coma," I whispered.

"Oh, you are not!" She laughed and ate some more Brussels sprouts. "Aren't these delicious?"

"No, not delicious," I gasped. "Sweet…far too sweet…"

"I know," she nodded sagely. "That's what makes them so good."

Now why, on God's green earth, would anyone put sugar on a vegetable? The brown sugar did not improve the Brussels sprouts, at all. The nasty concoction could have been put into a blender and then used to frost a cake. Whose idea was this? I think these hoity-toity chefs at these hoity-toity restaurants spend all their time dreaming up new ways to render ordinary foods unrecognizable.

I, on the other hand, stick to what I know. Vegetables are to be seasoned with salt and pepper, not sugar. Desserts contain sugar, not salt and pepper. Cigarette buns are not half bad when sprinkled with cinnamon.

***

There was a huge debate in my family about the origin of a dish my mom often made: kraut burgers. My dad, being Czech, said they came from Czechoslovakia. My little friends at school told me they came from Germany. When I passed this information on to my dad, it did not go over well. I learned another new word.

***

Living in the Midwest, I have seen horrible things done to food, things that are just sacrilegious. For example, some people have interpreted sushi with far too much artistic license. I was looking at some sushi behind the glass window of the deli, debating whether I should buy it, and I noticed that it had a suspicious sauce on it. I asked the helpful-looking Asian man behind the counter, "What is that sauce on the sushi?"

"It's spicy sauce," he said, proudly.

"Um, what exactly is in the spicy sauce?" I asked, uneasily. He stared at me blankly.

"It's spicy sauce," he said again.

Okay, I see what's going on here. This man has been sworn to secrecy by management not to reveal the ingredients of the spicy sauce, just as KFC will not reveal what the eleven herbs and spices are on its chicken, and Coca-Cola will not reveal the recipe for Coke. Okay, I get it.

I decided to buy the sushi, because I was really hungry and I love sushi. At home, I took a big bite. I discovered that the spicy sauce consisted of about ninety-eight percent mayonnaise, and two percent something spicy, which could not be identified, because the mayonnaise canceled the flavor of the spice. It also very effectively canceled the flavor of the sushi. In fact, there was no detectable sushi flavor whatsoever in the sushi. I simply had a mouthful of mayonnaise.

After a lot of gagging and spitting, I recovered enough to get a damp napkin and carefully wipe off the remaining spicy sauce from the rest of the sushi. I should have just thrown the whole lot into the trash can, but I am a cheapskate. The removal of the mayonnaise rendered the sushi almost edible. Not quite, but almost.

I was left with many questions. Who decided that mayonnaise was an acceptable sauce to put on sushi? If someone, through his own volition, actually *wants* to put mayonnaise on sushi, cannot that person ruin, I mean, alter, his own sushi at home? Is the International Commission on Purity of Sushi aware of what is going on in this Midwest grocery store?

I am truly at a loss for words as to the reasoning behind what I experienced that day. There are certain things that simply are not done. Pulled pork is not served at a bar mitzvah. Sardines are not used to garnish an angel food cake. Mayonnaise is not squirted on sushi.

I did eventually go back to that store. I smiled at the Asian man behind the counter. "See this tray of sushi here? Yes, that one. Can you make me one just like that, without the sauce?"

He seemed perplexed. Clearly, no one had ever asked this question before. "You don't want the spicy sauce?" he asked. I think he must have thought that he misheard me.

"Yes, that's correct," I smiled politely. "I would like some plain sushi, without mayonnaise. Please."

He frowned. "Okay, but it will take about ten minutes. Come back in ten minutes."

"No problem," I smiled again. It was worth ten minutes to get some unadulterated sushi.

I took my newly-made sushi home and slathered it with wasabi and ginger, the only acceptable spicy sauce allowed on sushi.

Politics

I do not like the Re-Puke-icans or the Demo-Rats.
I do not trust them. I am a person of Action. I like
to get things done. Many scientific studies have
proven, beyond a doubt, that this does not happen
in politics.

I, for one, do not understand this. If I did not get
anything done at my job, I would not have a job.
Yet the Pukes and the Rats continue getting paid
for throwing up on and giving fleas to one another,
and doing absolutely no other form of detectable
work.

Both parties seem bent on delaying everything as
long as they possibly can, if not until next year,
then until the next election. They cannot agree on
anything, except for one very important thing.
Both parties agree emphatically that our nation
should be trillions and trillions of dollars in debt.

I don't even know what a trillion is. How does one
define trillion? If I saw a trillion, I wouldn't
recognize it. I would probably call animal control.

"Hello, Animal Control? There's a trillion in my
back yard. I don't know how it got there; it wasn't
there yesterday. Can you come and get it, please?"

Alternative medicine

I decided to try acupuncture. I am of the mindset that I will try anything once. The book I had read on acupuncture promised freedom from pain, constipation, dandruff, depression, acne, fallen arches, and a whole bunch of other things that people would like to be free from, so I thought, why not?

The acupuncturist was very friendly and knowledgeable – too knowledgeable. She began telling me about meridians and release points, and used many other terms that acupuncturists use that the general public does not understand. I tried to listen but found my mind wandering. I probably should have listened.

"Now, lie down on the exam table and take a few deep breaths," she instructed me. "I am going to insert the first needle along the whatsit meridian, and the second needle along the whosit meridian. The third and fourth needles will be inserted in the wheresit and whysit meridians."

My whatsit meridian began bleeding, coincidentally, when the first needle was inserted. The pain of having my meridians penetrated by very sharp needles had not been explained in the book. In fact, I'm pretty sure that the book had stated something like, "Acupuncture, when done properly, is virtually painless."

That word "virtually" could be interpreted a couple of different ways. As in, if you receive a "virtual" acupuncture session, done online, by a "virtual" acupuncturist, it will be "virtually" painless. Duh!

"Um, I'm bleeding," I told the acupuncturist timidly.

"That is just the release of toxins from your body," she said firmly.

"Funny how toxins look so much like blood," I whispered faintly. She wiped away the toxins with a tissue, then left the room and said she would be right back.

It was a good thing that I was already lying down, because I started to see spots dancing below the ceiling that was swirling into a misty pattern, then re-solidifying. I decided it was best to close my eyes.

The knowledgeable lady came back into the room several times, to rotate the needles. Each time she did this, it jolted me back to consciousness from the pain-induced coma I had slipped into.

After thirty minutes, my session was finally over. I got up from the table, got dressed, and hobbled out. I did not feel less toxin-laden than I had felt when I first arrived. After carefully evaluating the pros and cons of acupuncture, I decided that this type of alternative medicine was not for me. However, I did read a book on medicinal mushrooms, so…

Driving

I started teaching Zach how to drive when he was very young. That's how my mammy and pappy done fer me, and that's how I done fer my youngun'. I figured it would be a good idea for him to know how to reach over and grab the wheel in case I had some kind of medical emergency.

We began this grand experiment on the way home from a big city. Instead of taking the freeway, I pulled off onto a desolate country road, and told Zach it was time for him to learn. Now, you would think most kids would be eager to learn how to drive. Not Zach.

"I'm too young to drive!" he said, panicked, when I told him to switch places with me. "What if something happens?"

"Everybody has to learn how to drive sometime," I said soothingly. "Better now than later."

Twenty minutes later, we still hadn't moved. My eyes had begun to glaze over after the fortieth question about the interior of the car. "And what is this little knob for? And why does it have a red dot in the middle? And what is this black thing with the lever on it?"

"Zach!" I said finally, exasperated. "You don't need to know what every doo-hickey on the dashboard is for! Just fasten your seatbelt and put your foot on the gas!"

He obeyed. The car crept forward slowly. "You're doing fine," I reassured him. The car leaped forward with a sudden burst of speed. "Okay, brake!" I shouted. He braked. Both our heads snapped forward and back. "Okay, deep breath," I smiled at him. He began hyperventilating.

"Mom, I don't like this," he frowned. "What if I wreck your car?"

"You won't wreck my car," I assured him. "We're on a gravel road with no other cars, and you are going to drive very slowly. You're doing great! Only twenty more miles till we hit the highway again, and I'll take over from there."

"Twenty more miles?! We could both be dead by then!"

I wonder why Zach is so dramatic. No one else in my family is dramatic. Certainly not I. I am calm, cool, collected and level-headed at all times. I did not panic when I fell off the treadmill. I did not over-react when I had to spit the mayonnaise-covered sushi out of my mouth.

"No one is going to die on this trip," I said firmly. "You are going to learn how to drive. When I am old, I am going to call you and you are going to come pick me up and drive me to the grocery store, to the doctor, to the hair salon, to the Very Muscular Men's gym – "

He stepped on it again. Somehow, we made it to the highway in fits and starts. Side note: I had never understood the expression "fits and starts" until I gave my son a driving lesson.

When we got home, Zach jumped out of the car and raced into the house. I entered the living room in time to hear the words, - "and she forced me to drive! I'm never driving again! I hate driving!" He then raced to his room and slammed the door.

Hub looked at me over the top of his glasses. "He's too young to drive," he noted.

I rolled my eyes. "Oh, what's the big deal? He drove for twenty miles on a gravel road, and he did fine. I'm proud of him."

"I think you may have traumatized him for life," Hub said. "He may never be able to drive again."

Well, that was then. Zach is a lot older now, and I don't see much of him, because he's always off driving somewhere.

Did I mention that he was eight when I gave him the driving lesson on the gravel road?

***

Come to think of it, I myself have been traumatized for life by driving. I also hate driving! But, sadly, I am forced to drive most places. It is not so much the act of driving itself that bothers me, it's the actions of the other people on the road. There are the texters, the musicians, the yellers, the gesticulators, the swervers, the bewildered, and the elderly.

Texters

At every red light their chins are on their chests. They look up hurriedly every now and then, then drop their gaze again. I get stuck behind them sometimes, which is not as bad as being perpendicular to them. They are unpredictable.

Musicians

They beat out a rhythm on the steering wheel. If the window is down, you can hear them singing. They bob up and down in their seats, bouncing, singing, banging on the steering wheel. They love to share their music with everyone on the street.

You will know you are next to a musician because your windows will rattle.

Yellers

They may be yelling at you, or at the person they are riding with. Yellers sometimes punctuate their yells with quaint hand signals. I had a yeller behind me once who was tailgating while yelling. He let me know that I was number one, but neglected to use his index finger, as is customary. I responded by blowing kisses at him. He then became a swerver.

Gesticulators

Not all gesticulators are conveying anger, although most are. I have seen some pointing at scenery, clapping their hands, giving a thumbs-up, and shaking their fists. I once saw a gesticulator – thankfully a passenger – giving her impression of a tree blowing in the wind. It was quite entertaining.

Swervers

No one knows why swervers swerve so much. Maybe they just get bored by driving in a straight line. Maybe their car is filled with the odor of an overflowing diaper. Maybe there is a bee in the car. Who knows?

The bewildered

I have been bewildered while driving a time or two, myself. *Isn't this Sandra's house? I'd better slow down. It looks like Sandra's house, but it's a different color. Oh, there's someone behind me – sorry! Just go around.*

Maybe Sandra lives on the next block. Is that a Great Pyrenees? You don't see many of those. Oops – when did this street become a one-way? Sorry – just go around me.

The elderly

I try to have patience with the elderly. But really, there comes a day to turn in the car keys.

Elderly people drive *very slowly*. There's nothing wrong with being cautious, but elderly people turn on their turn signals five miles before they are ready to turn. Elderly people look left, look right, look left again, look right again, and oops! the light's red now, and there's a whole lot of yelling and gesticulating going on in the car behind.

The long arm of the law

I have been stopped for speeding too many times. Once, I was pregnant, and I actually toyed with the idea of telling the officer that I was in labor and on the way to the hospital, but decided that this might backfire on me. On that occasion, I had to go to STOP class. I did not enjoy it. One, I was the only pregnant person in the class. Two, I was the only person over thirty in the class. Three, it took up most of my Saturday, which I had designated for other things.

We had to do a self-evaluation in this class. On a scale of one to ten, we were supposed to decide how good of a driver we were. This is a hilarious evaluation to give to a class full of people who have broken the law. I circled "four" and gave my paper back to the instructor. She gathered all the papers into a neat stack, and then frowned. "Who circled four?" she asked.

"I did," I said, raising my hand politely.

"I think you have a problem with self-esteem," she said soothingly. "Don't worry; you're in the right place."

I was not sure how my self-esteem would improve while being in a room full of law-breakers, but I'll try anything once. I answered all the questions, watched the video, and took the final test. I even wrote a neat little essay on the test. In the essay, I explained how people with size eleven feet were more likely to speed than those with smaller feet. I asked for the instructor's leniency, due to this genetic condition that I had no control over.

I did pass the class. As I was leaving at the end of the day, I noticed the instructor staring at my feet. "Wow, you weren't kidding," she said.

I smiled politely. "No, I wasn't kidding. I really do have big feet, but they give me a good understanding."

No one gets that joke, but I think it's funny.

The next time I was stopped for speeding, I had a fourteen-month old baby strapped in a car seat in the back. I thought, *"Surely, the officer will take pity on me."* He didn't. This guy was all business. He didn't crack a smile the whole time he was writing me a ticket. This, despite the fact that Zach was yelling from the back seat, over and over, "Hi, Mr. Policeman! Hi, Mr. Policeman!" Not only did the officer not smile, I thought I detected the hint of a frown.

I turned around and put my index finger to my lips. "Ha, ha; yes, Zach, there's a nice policeman here (shhhh!!!). He's here to help us; that's what the police do (shhhh!!!).

Who can resist a cute baby yelling, "Hi, Mr. Policeman! Hi, Mr. Policeman?" This guy, apparently. He wrote me a "nice" ticket. That's how I described it to Zach, anyway.

The officer got back in his car, frowning, and drove away. I also drove away, clutching my brand-new speeding ticket. I took off my shoes, reasoning that this would make my feet slightly smaller, thus enabling me to drive at the speed limit.

I really don't want any further brushes with the law. They are embarrassing. I have learned that I can embarrass myself quite easily without any help from the police.

Why?

Why is it ever necessary, under any circumstances, to bring an unsilenced cell phone into church?

Why do you have to enter your account number on the phone keypad, then verbally tell the human being your account number again?

Why do they ask you to buy an extended warranty for an item made of cardboard?

Why do children's movie tickets cost less than adults'?

Why do people put fertilizer on their grass, then complain when they have to mow the lawn?

Why do desserts have so many calories, yet when you read the ingredients, "calories" is not listed anywhere?

May your life be filled with laughter and non-stop nonsense.

Julia Anshasi
2020

www.ingramcontent.com/pod-product-compliance
Lightning Source LLC
LaVergne TN
LVHW041231080426
835508LV00011B/1158